About the Author

D. L. Arber, writer, actor and poet, was born in Illinois and grew up in Colorado. He is a 2005 graduate of the University of Northern Colorado in Theatre Arts. As a student he performed in numerous school productions and also participated in New York University's summer theatre program. Following graduation he worked on stage, both as an actor and a producer, and in television in New York and Los Angeles, before returning to Colorado. In recent years he has been involved in writing short stories and poetry, political works and now this book on schizophrenia.

"This is My Playground" is a book on the experiences and feelings of author, poet and actor D. L. Arber. Previously on television and the stage, David's work here is focused on mental illness.

Currently living in Colorado after time spent growing up in Illinois, NYC and Los Angeles, David's "This is My Playground" shares with the reader many experiences he has had through the years of suffering from the mental illness schizophrenia.

This is My Playground:

My Fight with Schizophrenia

By

D. L. Arber

Contents

How it Happened

When I was little, I discussed with my parents whether or not to go to a rodeo or to go ice skating. It was the middle of autumn and I was worried I might be trampled by the crowd either way, and I had never been ice skating so I thought it would be the perfect opportunity to try something new. It was my father and I who decided to skip the rodeo and I was given the opportunity to make the final decision to pick between the two. I picked ice skating. The fact that I never had been and the allure of the Olympics and perhaps the girls I would meet there, and it just seemed like I would be doing something instead of just sitting back and watching something happen, made me all the more interested. It has been quite some time since that day and I remember it, in little spots and pictures, as I remember a fireplace where I was spending time at over at the friends of the families and then I remember some of us wearing turtlenecks where it was cooling down becoming fall-like~in~ the weather. What's funny is I don't really remember the actual ice skating event, almost like it never happened. What I remember is being asked what I wanted to do. I am pretty certain we attended the ice skating center that evening and enjoyed ourselves and perhaps we even fell a few times on the ice with the rented skates that we had. What I remember is important, as my memories always seem to come in little bits and in small increments, unless of course it was a large event, but in this case it was a simple outing we had and for this I got to choose.

This happened when I was around three to four years old and I can barely recall what led us to doing anything more that evening except skating around on the ice and maybe getting a hamburger from the local concession stand. The point was that it was an easy environment to spend the time, and not a rough and tough event where I would be around people with alcohol and what I didn't want to be around. Events like these stay in my mind and have been with me since I was a child, and many of these are thankfully unharmed by the outside world and the danger a child can be put in at young age. Thankfully there were two people who would care for me in the coming years: my parents. The important thing is that I remember details like this sometimes when I am thinking back on the years I have lived.

When I was younger I spent a lot of time arguing with my parents. I can't tell you exactly what about, but for example, I would argue about what I wanted to eat for a meal, or I would argue about what kind of clothing to buy, or I would argue about what to do on the weekend and even who to spend time with. I think I always wanted to spend time with friends outside of the family because it gave me a chance to get more acquainted with people I didn't know that well, and it gave me a chance to learn about others. I would meet a friend at school and I would get a chance to hang out with them after school or on a weekend. I never got into too much trouble either, I usually had good judgment.

When I was young and even through elementary school until about grade six I was in a safe environment under my parent's wing until one day I would begin junior high school and the seventh grade. I did pretty well in school up until then, learning the basics of math and writing, English language, social studies and history. I don't think there was a time during my elementary years that I didn't have someone watching over me while I did my homework in the afternoon, or when I learned a problem at school or read a poem in language class while standing in front of everyone. I am not sure what school programs are like these days, as I have been out of the classroom for nearly 10 years now. Things I remember of course were chalkboards or cubby holes or coat racks that lined the walls and I remember desks and books and posters on the walls of great places like the Great Wall of China or the Grand Canyon.

When I entered seventh grade is when I would attend a school that was a bit more public than my elementary school and I was enrolled in a place where the population of students was made up of people throughout the neighborhood. The people in junior high school came from much more varied backgrounds than I, so sometimes I would feel like I fit in, and other times, I felt that the pursuance of gangs, violence and drugs became an undertone of the landscape in the school where I attended. Thankfully it wasn't severe, but much of the time I began to feel alone as I attended school and was pressured with learning such a vast array of ideas. I know now that we were given that much knowledge at an early age because at that time we could hold it all down and learn it all, and soak it in.

As I learned more and more through the hard work given to the students at my junior high school I spent a lot of time meeting new people, and getting used to the work, but I had a hard time getting all of the information correct. There was always a lot to learn and as I grew older, there were pressures on people at school to conform and to be a part of a group to fit in, and for me I really didn't know where my friends were. I thought it was the people who wore all of the sports attire, and the logos and the expensive clothing. I thought it was the people who smoked the cigarettes after school or the people who made a scene and got into trouble. You see, those were the people that stood out, those were the ones that made the headlines in a school newspaper or were the talk of the hallway between classes. I wouldn't say I was distracted, but I would find myself among the ones that had an inkling to get in trouble in some way, or break a school rule somehow.

During school, and attempting to learn the subjects I had to through school, I began having social problems and began having issues with people once I began to learn different parts of the playground and learning about people, I began to rebel a little bit and branch out on my own. When I began to learn more about myself, I started to find things I didn't like, things I didn't want to live with and I didn't have the coping skills to understand it all and deal with it in a healthy way.

This is when my mother thought it was a good idea to become acquainted with a psychologist outside of school who I could talk to about my problems with life, people and school. This would be someone I could go to and get help understanding why I was having certain problems with people where it was having an interference with my school work and normal day to day life. Junior high school would end between two and three p.m. and I would be excited to go home; and living nearby I would even walk. Most of the time I was picked up by my mother at around two forty five and we would make our way home and talk about school that day. The psychologist sort of became the middle man between my work, school and home life. It was a place where I could discuss me and the issues I was having at the present time. My mother would take me there after school once every 3 weeks or so.

I began attending these appointments and discussing my issues with the psychologist and became a happier and healthier individual. The more the psychologist spoke with me and I discussed the issues I was having with people and school, soon the psychologist would come up with a diagnosis. I would be diagnosed with oppositional defiant disorder. When I was younger, I really had no idea what that meant, nor did I have any idea as to how it would affect my life, nor did I really understand what it was. I would come to know it better as I got older and had more experiences with it. But when I was that age, it was just the beginning.

When I Knew

As I stated in the previous chapter, I first learned that I had a bit of a problem and mental disability when around the seventh grade. At that time, I began seeing a psychologist and learning about the problems and differences I would have with other people, work, school and home life. I would find that by knowing more about myself, I could interact with the world better and understand others too. It wasn't by any means severe, and it wasn't suggested to prescribe medication=until many years later which is when I decided to finally seek medical treatment. Since the seventh grade I would spend a lot of my time doing homework, and being alone, and I found it difficult to do things a lot of the time because I was around so many different types of people from all walks of life. I didn't really think much of it, but I found that there were many people that were dependent on others at that age, and I found myself becoming more and more dependent on myself growing up. Looking back, I think different problems came up as there was more and more peer pressure to be like other people rather than simply do what I wanted to do, like the beginning, being able to choose what I liked and wanted from life. This would become an important part of what makes me who I am today.

Knowing I actually had a mental illness didn't come to me until I was in my mid twenties when I was attending college and couldn't handle things on my own. In grade school, I found that there were would be conflicts with teachers and other students because what I expected from them, they couldn't provide, and I suppose it wasn't really my place to ask. From seventh grade on I would see a psychologist on a regular basis in and out of going to and from school. I don't think there was ever really a problem so severe that it couldn't be helped, because we could take the time to step out of our normal environment and assess what the problem was before it got too far out of control.

Seventh and eighth grade didn't really go well on the spectrum of learning. I spent a lot of time behind in class and trying to keep up with everyone and the teachers. Too much time was wasted and I think there was a chance that I really didn't learn the material. Some of this may have been due to the fact that I may have had some disability from a young age and not known it. I failed eighth grade, and because of that my parents pulled me out of public school and put me into a private college preparatory school that had fewer students, and was a more hands-on learning experience. We didn't attribute the lack of good grades to any mental illness at that time; it was just a desire to get things moving again so I would have a better life for myself and do well in school. The public school was full of different walks of life and a lot of the real world, but then there wasn't a specific focus for kids, just a curriculum that was followed by the teachers. The private school I was put into in the ninth grade would change my direction in a number of different ways, and for the better.

After failing the eighth grade I was enrolled in The Colorado Springs School in the mountains of Colorado and I would be given an education that was different and more specific than that of a public education. For one, I was given a hands-on approach to learning, and in classes of no more than 15 I would attend and learn a variety of different skills and studies. I am not sure if this had any effect on me mentally, but surely it gave me a larger spectrum of topics learned and also a viewpoint that I was important and not just another student that would make his way through the halls. I was treated in a way that was more direct and focused to how I learned and listened to for my own opinions and ideas. This was perhaps a place that would work with any disability I may have had, but there was no new diagnosis at that time.

As the ninth grade came I would be exposed to different programs at The Colorado Springs School that I wouldn't have access to if I was left to survive in a public school. Because of my low grades in the seventh and eighth grade I would have to have to have some special consideration in admittance for the school, something I either had to provide through essay or through a meeting with specific school teachers, so we both would understand what is at stake when being admitted to the college preparatory school. It was the schooling I needed that I would propel me in the direction I took after high school and would lead to the difference I needed to survive in the real world.

I spent four years in high school and graduated in the early summer of 1996. At that time, mentally I was feeling like I had accomplished something good, I had worked my way through four years of high school and I had worked hard at my courses, writings and had decided on a private college for my first year of post high school education. One thing that I would become involved in would be the high school theatre program where I would star in school productions. I had a lot of different classes, but when other people would go off after school to do sports or to their education groups; I was getting involved in school theatre productions in the local cafeteria and the theatre they had built there my sophomore year. Productions like *Grease, Tartuffe, Little Shop of Horrors and Arsenic*

and Old Lace were just a few of the
productions I would star in as an actor in the
high school productions. I had no problem with
enjoying the art and being a part of a play
production there that would shape my coming
years as an artist, an actor and a person.

I didn't really come to recognize or
understand that I had a mental illness until I
was in my twenties while I was in college.
When I began college the first time, I was put
up in dorm rooms where I would meet a whole
variety of different people and I would begin
to learn about them and myself. I didn't have
the control over my life as I did in high school,
being close to a home environment like
parents and friends. When I moved, I lived in a
dormitory not too far from school and I would
travel each day to and from to learn. As a first
year freshman, I suppose there would be some
differences I would have with the students,
being from another state, and having a

different upbringing. However I would have different things that I would learn about myself that would affect my decisions in the future, and have an effect on my coping skills. Dealing with so many people that had a liking to extra curricular drugs and alcohol was one of the first things I was exposed to in a college environment. Growing up I was not brought up to drink and do drugs in or around the home. Growing up I spent the majority of time with animals or listening to music. In high school I starred in the school plays and the first year I spent in college, I would star in the school theatre production, an extension of what I accomplished and did in high school. I had become involved in the theatre arts system regularly in high school and each year I would audition and ended up performing in the school plays. In college it was a bit different; however for the year there I seemed to have a talent for acting and performing art, so I stuck with it as I left the first year with a starring role under my belt.

It was a private college that I attended, and when I left I had my reasons, but there were some conflicts with being so far away from family. If I remember correctly, I had only gone to school there for one year. After I left, I came back to Colorado where I began attendance at a state university. There I would formally begin my college education. I had a wide range of classes and I would also be a part of a theatre program there and get involved in a number of productions.

At this time, I had no real problems with mental health and I had no encounters with people regarding mental illness. I was doing fine. It wasn't until after I returned as a student the second time after taking a three year break from college to pursue my career as an actor would I have problems in the realm of psychology. I spent a summer studying acting at NYU and then, in 1999, I decided to leave school in Colorado and pursue an acting career in California. I moved to the San Fernando Valley in late 1999 and found a place to live. I would spend the next three years working as an actor on television, theatre and film. It was what I wanted to do as a career in life and I never had any issue with any mental problems at that time. I do remember having seen a psychologist at that time in California. I spent some time there working and playing and also at that point, I would see a psychologist to talk about my problems and issues I was having in work and anything with people. I would see this psychologist once a month at an office and speak about these things. It became a habit and sort of regularity to see a psychologist and speak about these things. It helped, when I was living in such a large city.

As time went on, I spent time acting a lot. Along with acting came the development of characters I would make up, whether it was for a role, or for something I wrote. Creating a character was one thing I would learn how to do in acting classes there and I would understand how to develop different people and personalities to fit what I was working on. Along with doing this, I needed to stay grounded within myself to know exactly where I was coming from and from what part of myself I was drawing these characters. As part of learning about these plays and playwrights I was studying in classes, I was still seeing a psychologist. The psychologist never prescribed me medication, but I had talked about perhaps thinking about trying something to help with my nervousness and irritability when around other people. To this day I still have some irritability or impatience being around certain types of people who don't seem to have what I need or want to be around. This is because I know where I am coming from going into many different situations=is similar to a student going into a classroom.

In the Beginning

In the beginning of my illness I refused treatment. I would be okay with seeing a psychologist, but was against taking a pill for my illness. Up into my twenties, I saw a psychologist regularly in and out of school and I spent a lot of time talking and learning about how I felt among other people. I wanted to find out where I fit, and what I could do the best. I found myself in acting school, in bartending academies and working side jobs to make money, but I always was around other people who were working to support their own lives. A restaurant job was a great job for an actor, because not only did it keep you interacting with people, it kept you on your toes and feet walking around with people. In 2003, after working for three years in California, I decided it was time to get back to school as I had outspent myself in shows and plays in the theatre district there. It was then I decided to move back to Colorado to finish my Bachelors of Arts degree in Performing Art, with an Emphasis in Acting. Moving back to Colorado after experiencing what it was like to be a working actor, I would have some problems with getting back into a school setting among students of all vocations.

When I was first in a medical setting, I was diagnosed with schizophreniform disorder, and I said no to treatment for a number of reasons. For one, I didn't want to have to take a pill. I think many kids of all ages will agree with me when I say taking a pill before bedtime is an annoying occurrence. I really didn't think about it all that much, I just felt like being stubborn like many people my age. At that time, in my early twenties after spending years on my own in Los Angeles, I felt that I really knew everything there was to know about life. I didn't need a medical doctor telling me I needed to take a pill to help me mentally. I felt it was my responsibility and I was halfway successful so I didn't want to jeopardize anything that I knew about myself. I also didn't want to admit I had any disorder.

In my first year back as a student in Colorado as a junior in college was when I had a problem with a counselor where I told him I had been angry about people around me and was worried about the decisions I had made so far in life coming back to finish school. I had left a life that was hard enough as it is to be an artist and actor where I had to get financial help to put my productions on and how it was fairly difficult to get to and from auditions and set in a huge city of Los Angeles. I had found a counselors office on campus and, from what I told him, I think he perceived me to be a threat on campus. He called campus police and had me admitted to a local hospital where it was suggested that I be put on a medication called Serequel. It was a type of antipsychotic drug that was supposed to work in the treatment of schizophrenia and bipolar disorder. They tried to get me to use it when I was admitted to the hospital, but I refused.

I believe I refused, because growing up I really never had to take medication for anything more than a cold. I don't really believe I was refusing treatment because I didn't want to get better; it was just because I didn't like taking a pill. Like any child, I don't want to be affected by something that is not natural and organic. I felt that putting a pill in my system was not going to make me any better and any healthier. I believe I spent an overnight there, being evaluated, where I would learn what my actions would mean on a broader scale and what consequences they could lead me to. In retrospect, I feel that going through that made me realize what these serious comments would mean in a situation like that.

I got more stubborn about medication as I learned that it would affect my mind. I was afraid that there would be a problem if I took the medication and something would go wrong. I didn't want to be stuck with a mental breakdown or a mental mix up of some kind while taking some kind of pill, and not understanding what could happen if I was out of control of my life. I was afraid that the pill was going to put me out of control. After being offered the Serequel at that time, I refused to take it and went home the next day with my family, who had to drive 100 miles up to the university campus to come and get me. It was something I won't forget, and the time spent there would give me a broader understanding of what I was up against as far as my mental health.

Still, it would be many years later before I would begin to take the medication that I am currently on, that I would decide that I would try to take anything to make me healthier mentally I was first hospitalized in 2003, and I had returned to finish my degree in college. Now, nearly ten years later, I have just begun to take a medication called Risperidone. It is another antipsychotic drug that while taking I have noticed some differences in my life. I suppose I would say it has brought me back to me, and given me a clear mind and helped my thinking process. When I returned to Colorado after living in New York City for three years, I found that taking the medication in a safe environment where I was distant from crime or out of the way of stress, that it helped me in a number of ways and has given me more freedom of thought and life, and helped me put my priorities in order.

Another reason I refused treatment was due to the reason that for most of the people administering the drugs, and the people that are working in these health care facilities, I didn't trust. I don't normally trust someone the second I meet them, let alone let them prescribe me medication. At least that is what I thought to begin with. I know these people have medical degrees and have a license to administer drugs of these sorts, but I didn't feel like I could trust them at any rate. So, I felt there wasn't going to be a chance I trusted these professionals any further than I could throw them, which wasn't that far.

When I saw a psychologist for my years as a teenager and into my twenties, I developed trust over time with them. Just like any relationship, you come to know these people and understand their way of life, so I would soon begin to understand and develop my own relationship with them and then feel comfortable to speak with them about the issues I was having. I never saw a psychologist again until I was in my thirties and I was having some different changes occur which I didn't expect, and that came with age. For example, as a person in my thirties, I have traveled a bit, worked for a few different employers, as I was in the entertainment industry and in a way outsourced to the different projects that were available at the time for an actor. I really didn't spend a lot of time in a chair at a psychologist's office. But it was at the concern of my family that I did-I go back into treatment, so I would bring attention to the problems I had had throughout the years and I would begin to bring them to light. Working, throughout my twenties and living in different cities gave me the experience I needed to understand what was appropriate in real life as what I needed to be self sufficient. I also gained common knowledge of the industry I was working in, and began to understand what was important and what wasn't.

What I Notice

As I moved from being against the treatment of antipsychotic drugs, to being more aware and understanding they may actually play a positive effect in my life, I began to notice a lot of changes in my life when I began to take the medication. First, I want to go through what a typical day would be like before I began the meds, and tell you what I experienced. My diagnosis as a paranoid schizophrenic was only because, at least in my opinion and my view, due to the fact that I would have my own paranoid delusions in and about life. I can remember thinking, and sometimes having a problem with money because of the lack of care or low pay at the jobs I held. I went to school for art and acting and if I wasn't booking jobs as an actor, I wasn't working, and therefore not making any money. The paranoia came from having little money and not having the ability to pay rent, and also living in places that were run down, and not in decent working order. Because of low income I have had to settle for places that were not as well kept; this was another fear I developed. Instead of working my daily life as an actor, the problems of having a living and of having quality relationships became the focus rather than actually working and feeling confident with the position I was in.

When one is constantly worried about whether their house is going to be broken into at night, whether they have a roof over their head that doesn't leak, and also having to sleep in a rushed manner, not knowing what the next day will bring can leave some people disheveled to say the least. It is not a situation that is stable and strong, in fact it is exactly the opposite. I developed fears and paranoia based on what was going to break the next day, and the worries of life, like, how much I would be paying for such a run down low income apartment, or working at a job where I would have no control over what happened next and not be able to balance my schedule with my checkbook. I noticed changes in my mood, because I would become frustrated at things I couldn't control and I would ask myself, "Why am I even doing this in the first place?" In the beginning I felt that my profession came with breaks, and the work one put in would have an effect on the outcome of one's dream or salary. As a teenager, and even into my twenties, working as an actor was an enjoyable profession and I liked most of what I learned because of acting in a number of productions and knowing myself. What I also noticed is that in this type of profession I was the sole funding source for most of the projects I auditioned for, as I had a number of expenses as an actor that needed to be paid for in order to get into the profession. The mental worries didn't really come until I found myself not making the kind of money I wanted to make as an actor, and in turn had experiences that were not to be expected and couldn't be controlled. When things began to get out of control, I had to withdraw from the industry and make a decision to point myself in a direction where there was some more stability. I found that that returning to school helped me mentally and emotionally, but there was a fear of others that came from working in the acting industry because of the instability of the industry itself. When the industry is based on certain things like looks and style, I would find myself trying to fit into a mold that was not attainable. It was probably one of the reasons I left to finish college to begin with.

I would notice a change in life as I did something for myself, and for others. I found that if I wanted to better myself, I would have to make an effort to learn something new. I think when something gets stale and old, it doesn't offer any help to one's own worth or value. It only weakens what they came for in the first place. I notice my emotional changes when the imbalance in life comes with regular every day struggles getting out of control and are unable to be helped. When rent prices soar, for example and my pay as an actor stays low, it only increases the stress in one's mind and life. I began to notice that people of all professions may have the sense of change that I had at one point, but that living as an actor came with a lot of trouble when I wasn't working or couldn't make a living.

Certain changes in my life harbored illness. For example, when I had to move for work, it brought with it a lot of stress and struggle in getting to know new people and new places and having to try and survive under the struggle as an actor. Some jobs weren't available to me, and then when they weren't, paying for rent became difficult. I also felt that I would try so hard just to make a rent check that I would feel that I would be thinking about rent and safety all the time I was working instead of having fun and enjoying work. The more the rent prices were out of range of an actor's budget, the more I would struggle everyday just trying to make it all work. It was only me, and I only had my parents on my side, so the stress itself would get to me mentally. I think the stress of being an actor and working to become other people everyday only made me use myself even more and made me "stress out" sometimes. Most of the characters I played would have some emotional problems anyway, and I was always delving into what it was like "To Be" the character.

It was a good thing I saw a psychologist regularly as I would be able to "vent" what was on my mind about the troubles of the job or the specifics of the characters I was playing.

I have since taken a bit of a break from acting as I haven't been able to survive with the low pay that most places provide for a person that is simply looking for work, and not searching to be the next big thing, which by the way, I have noticed doesn't last. Also, I seemed to be type cast in some roles where the characters had emotional instability. And if I didn't look a certain way, which meant regular trips to the thrift store to find clothes that worked on set, then I wasn't cast. All that goes into the work as an actor can be daunting. It was fun for a while, but when you are always changing clothes to fit the mold of someone else's story, it can be difficult to survive.

In a sense this is probably "all in my mind" as could be said. I know one thing, as a person that would walk to the bus stop, or the subway stop in New York City on a rainy day or a sunny day, I would feel that it took me to make everything work, as I needed to be skilled in a number of areas to understand how to do a job, and being trained as an actor, I would get jobs that others wouldn't. However, it all came with a price. In a world full of entertainment, I found that there were avenues that were difficult to walk down, as I took it all on myself. I suppose the stress that came with my everyday work lent itself to my mental health, and it brought on stress factors about needing money, being in a competitive market and having to be on my feet or walk all day without much rest. These were factors that contributed to being tired. That coupled with a terrible infrastructure on the east coast, and having to worry about problems that would only fix themselves with proper funding, I found that the worries of everyday life overshadowed the desire to simply do work as an actor.

I lived in two different cities known for their entertainment. Los Angles and New York were where I tried to make it as an actor. The city of Los Angeles was much stronger and healthier when it came to living communities, and I felt is was easier to survive in Los Angeles without public transportation and driving to the places I needed. I don't know if you have ever ridden the bus in your town, but it can be a humbling and I would like to say, dirty experience. There are a number of different types of people on the busses and many of them harbor illnesses and are unclean. Moving across the country to New York, I found my living quarters to be old and out of shape. Having to work as an actor and dealing with an illness that I really hadn't noticed or understood, to set in, I would, on top of that, have to live in a place that perhaps had bugs, and didn't have strong working heat. These are the types of things that can have an effect on a mental state of a human being, and it did. Due to my illness, my perception of my surroundings often made it difficult to see reality clearly.

Hygiene, clean clothes, a clean bed and dry living space all contribute to a person's mental health. Living on low income for most of my adult life, I have seen the problems of the places I have lived and have come to know what to expect when your rent is what is marked as "affordable." I have found that renting apartments in different cities all come with a price and a different list of problems. I have encountered various issues that have affected me mentally and have taken the focus away from working as an actor and just simply working in general to afford a comfortable place to live and survive.

What is Important to Me

I was officially diagnosed with
schizophrenia in early March of 2014. Before
that I had seen a professional to assess my
current issues with life and they found that I
had a diagnosis when I was in my twenties. I
did some basic description of what I saw and
felt and what experiences I was having daily
like I described earlier and I found that these
problems that came with life affected me in a
way that could be treated medically.

Before I was diagnosed, I suppose I
didn't have enough money to even survive.
Now, I am on a fixed income and I have been
given a chance to change or fix some of the life
that I have. I have worked on myself mentally
and physically and tried to begin to eat
healthier. I have noticed that a shower is very
important to me along with cleanliness and

hygiene. I have found that being personally responsible for my possessions has helped me as well. I have noticed that taking public transportation doesn't work when you have to be somewhere at specific time. I also value clean food, and healthy food. I don't follow the food groups, as maybe I could, but these days it seems that there are so many different ways to eat, that one can become overwhelmed, but I know one thing is for sure, I stay away from fast food regularly. Only once a month or every few weeks do I indulge. Other things that are important to me at this time in my life are warmth, money, and family. I live close to home now so I can see them once a week. I find that a safe place away from crime is also important to me. I had different experiences while I was on the east coast where I had to watch out for myself, as there were people living close by that had criminal histories. Being close to these people, I actually had a time where a simple act of stealing my keys brought me to a police station where I had to report the crime. I believe it wouldn't have happened if I hadn't lived in a place where rent prices were "affordable." Finding a safe living place is a very important thing as I have found that if your safety is compromised while you sleep, then this is a situation that one should steer clear from. These are just some of the things that are important to me now that I am living with a disability.

Growing up, I didn't have to deal with crime in the house, and I wasn't subject to violence in my neighborhood where I lived, thankfully. Growing older, I have found that not all people had the upbringing that I did, and I am thankful for such. There are many people from different walks of life and who come from different places, and I believe that personal safety is of utmost importance when living and working. Growing up I have heard and seen the crime take place right in front of me on the screen and in the newspapers. Along with the select few friends I have had over the years I have come to understand that life really can be tough and survival is what it comes down to. I have never had everything, but I have grown up with a safe place to sleep and healthy food to eat. One should never take for granted what they have. Since I have been on my own I have had to do everything myself and I have found that many of the things that I have grown up with and have received, require money and always will. Foods, and a safe roof over one's head, are the main things that require me to spend. I wish it wasn't this way, but I guess there really isn't a way around it. These are things that are important to me. One thing that doesn't require money is simply being around family. Thankfully, just being with them doesn't require me to spend much; only a little on gasoline to get me there. Surely it has been said before, but family continues to stay important to me throughout the years.

I can say that I have found some things that continue to stay important to me, and many of those are free. Clean air to breathe, a nice walk outside, a dinner with family or friends, and a walk with my dog. I got a dog this year, and I find it important to have an animal or some kind of responsibility to something other than myself. Growing up and in high school I had fish and a fish tank that I could do a lot of things with and even put turtles or frogs in. I find the importance of being genuine with another human being to be helpful and worthwhile. Taking care of another individual is important too. I have been my own caretaker for many years up until now and have been okay. Being diagnosed with schizophrenia when I was a bit younger showed me what was important to me. When I found that I needed to do things on my own and there really wasn't any other way, I found that I wanted to do things I enjoyed, not things that made me feel constricted, or that would ultimately take my time and money. For example, if I had the chance to go out to a race car track or baseball game and spend hundreds of dollars vs. staying at home and enjoying something on television or in a book, knowing that the previous would cost a lot of money, I would choose to go the cheaper route. Also, things that were quieter and softer in a sense made helped me feel better than doing something that was abrasive and abrupt. Spending a quiet time at home rather than going out to spend a lot of money among a lot of loud people became more important to me. To this day, I watch my spending on things that don't make sense and ultimately don't provide any safety or security, but instead take it from you.

Recognizing that I felt more interested in quieting tasks, I found myself to enjoy things that were more grounded and not things that seemed to stretch me mentally and physically. It stemmed from understanding what using the money meant and what it took to achieve the things that it seems everyday American's do. After I was diagnosed I gave some time to stopping the acting process and relying on the basics and streamlining my daily activities to save money. While research shows that schizophrenia is a brain disorder that usually develops in early adulthood, I believe that people who are on a low, fixed income are more susceptible to mental illness. In fact I have found in some research that low income is a factor in getting treatment for mental illness, because of the fact that with less money, people don't have access to the quality care that could be provided if they were in a higher income bracket. A weak economy can contribute to illness. According to Vox.com, mental illness and economic problems are linked in a few ways. For one, being out of work hurts a person's sense of well-being and mental health. Being poor as a child can also affect a person's mental health. However, as shown in the study, "Schizophrenia is not usually because of a poor childhood." The study also suggests that mental illness and poverty can hurt upward mobility, and that education plays a large part in alleviating poverty. In a downward cycle, "if one is in poverty, more people are susceptible to illness."

That said, I can say that my education and career choice quite possibly have played a part in my development of schizophrenia. Not having adequate income as an adult, having a career that is at best hit or miss and requires long hours at different jobs to sustain the lifestyle, I have found that it is possible that my career choice may have not been the best when it comes to mental stability. This is not proven, but as I discussed earlier, moving to larger cities to find work, working in terrible conditions and being outside in the elements a lot of the time did contribute to my mental instability, and I did not have the patience to be at someone else's beck and call while I worked under these conditions. I found these conditions to be a contributing factor when it came to finding regular work and especially recently before returning home to Colorado, I found myself trying to make a living off of a day wage, which was nearly impossible. I can say from my own experience, when not having money and not being able to support oneself off of one's wage, I am saddened to say that what I loved to do have to be put on hold for some time until I was able to fund my way through it again. I have even said at times, that I would have to pay to work at these places. If I made one hundred dollars for the day as an actor, and my rental cost was eight hundred seventy five dollars, then I would have to work at least nine days out of the month just to support my rent. It was possible to do, but I found that many times there were so many people trying to work the same days I was, that it became hard to work the days I needed and to make the money to survive. So, with the struggle of money, life began to hurt me mentally and I had to find another way to live.

I suppose finding what is important to me comes in a bit of a of a cycle. What one needs to do and what one wants to do many times get confused. With me, in my twenties I began finding myself doing what I had to do to survive, whether my mental health was at stake or not. I don't think it should be that way, but I suppose one would argue that there should be a sacrifice in one's life to achieve the goals they desire. At the time, I felt that it wasn't a sacrifice I was willing to make when my health was at risk.

Doctors and Their Opinion

Over the time that I have been
involved with doctors, I have come to find that
no matter if I am seeing one or not for
whatever reason, they usually find something
to diagnose. In other words, if things are going
well in your life, I have found that a doctor will
find something to diagnose, whether it big or
small, and find a reason for something. This
time, things weren't going well. For the
diagnosis of schizophrenia, I was prescribed a
small amount of medication, only 2MG of the
drug Risperidone. I find it to be a small dose
and I am willing to live with it. The diagnosis
makes the mental illness really sort of non
existent in my life, as long as I take it once per
night as directed. I think a doctor will always
have an opinion about something and
whatever situation one is in, leave it to a
doctor to attempt to make do and fix it.

Schizophrenia is a mental illness that can be treated by the use of medication. When I was younger, I didn't receive medication. I didn't show major signs of the illness until I was in my twenties. I thought to myself at the time, that having a doctor prescribe me medication for something I wasn't really sure if I had or not, or being diagnosed for something that I really didn't know I had, or felt that I really didn't have, was a bit absurd. So, when a doctor comes along and tells you his opinion of what he or she sees or perceives, for me I was hesitant to go along with it and I refused any medication.

This may be because I have never really liked going to the doctor, and when I have it is usually because I don't feel well, sick or unhealthy. If I am to go to a doctor it is because of an illness a cough or a cold and I hope that he or she can find a reason for it so that it will be cured, vaccinated or made well. I suppose I really only need to go to the doctor when something is wrong, or I need some medication for something, or I have picked up something at school. God knows that when I would get a cold as a young person, it would be most often due to the people I would run into at school, the doorknobs I would touch, the unsanitary places I would be to pick up germs. But schizophrenia is not a germ, let's be firm on that, as it is really a disease of the brain, as scary as that sounds.

When I was first diagnosed as schizophrenic I relied on a psychologist to talk to and to suggest a way to get better. She would suggest different behaviors, different people to see, and different things to do to improve the problems in my life. There was a lot of validity to that, but the psychologists I had never prescribed medication because, as you may know, they are not supposed to. It wasn't until my thirties when I was given the referral to a local mental health facility that housed internal psychiatrists where I would be prescribed medication for my diagnosis. It was long after I graduated college. It was after I spent time in other cities trying my work as an actor and artist. So, it wasn't until then that I received medical treatment along with a place to talk about my concerns and troubles and problems with a psychologist all under one roof.

It is not that I have any problem with doctors. I just feel that their sole reason for existence is to find a reason or a cause and to help a person to get the care they need. These are good things; it is just, that when I am asked specific questions pertaining to my mental well being, how I perceive the world, if I am thinking about harming others, I know that I need to disclose that information to her. I always feel threatened by doctors who see many patients a day and on a general scale rely on the specifics of what a patient tells them to provide appropriate care. I suppose there are a number of ways to diagnose an individual, which is fine; I just feel like there should be a better way, especially when it could be the generalized methods that these hospitals use to give appropriate care to individuals.

Thankfully I don't have to see a doctor daily or weekly for that matter. I know that somewhere out there, there are people that have to see a doctor weekly or frequent the hospital on a daily basis for care, but I wouldn't want to be one of those people and I'm happy that I'm not.

Thankfully, I haven't had any problems with the care I have received, which is a positive thing. I haven't had any problems with the doctors I have seen for my illness. If I was in a place that gave me inappropriate care, I would certainly not continue seeing them.

The experiences I have had with the doctors I have seen since I have been diagnosed have been helpful and given me the care I needed to stay on the right track, or put me in the right direction. However, I sort of never realized I was going the wrong direction until I started seeing a psychologist. I suppose with their direction and listening skills, these doctors have given me a place to start from when finding the right direction to take. In the end, a doctor's opinion matters to me.

Psychologists and Psychiatrists

As you probably know, there is a difference between psychologists and psychiatrists. I have known this for most of my adult life, only because I spent the majority of the time going to see a psychologist, to simply talk about issues, problems and life. The latter, a psychiatrist, actually is there to prescribe a medication to a patient. I have been around psychologists more often than psychiatrists because my illness was never severe enough that I needed medication for it. In 2005 I graduated college after having taken time off to pursue my career, and the simple act of returning was daunting and sort of maddening only because of what I had known before hand, having just begun as a freshman five years earlier. A lot had changed just taking off three years. There were reasons for this, primarily because I felt that the trust factor with people got a lot lower as I began to run into more people who were from all walks of life. I began to be more aware of what life was like outside of school. Regardless, I had given myself years outside of school to work and live and it had given me experience that some other people hadn't got. When returning to school, I had learned a lot more about the industry and myself as a whole.

I moved back home and then into a small apartment where I found myself a job at a local restaurant, until I began to have problems with the management and patrons. I wasn't in care at the time, and I found myself working and buying a new car, and getting my life on track. It was good because I spent my time doing things, staying active and keeping out of trouble. I wasn't seeing a psychologist or a psychiatrist. I was just living and working. It was a decent time and I didn't feel like I needed any psychological help as I had control of the things I needed to in life. Having a decent work, life balance was something that I achieved at that time. As I lived and worked, I found that if I stayed on top of things, that I achieved what I needed and things stayed under control.

It wasn't until I lost my job as a waiter for having a complaint as a server that things sort of went downhill. I had a decent job making decent money, and then one day I rubbed a patron the wrong way and she complained and just then I was let go. I had some problems up to then with management and disregarding policy. It seemed that when I was working for myself, I would do fine, but when other people came into play, there would be issues between them because their policies would go against mine. I always looked at a job as just that, a job. I never looked at working for a restaurant as a career, which many people in that line of work did. I didn't really take a lot of other people's feelings into consideration; I was just trying to survive after graduating college.

Before college when I was young, I saw psychologists for my issues, and after college I didn't see anyone until after I returned home from my final trip to New York City in 2013. Between 2005 and 2013 were years which I would work, and attempt to make money and have a difficult time in getting things together. Choosing a field in art and performance didn't work unless I was in a city where there were performances, a place where one had an avenue to express one's self. Also, I found it very difficult to fund my own way to make it as an actor, as I needed those side jobs to make anything else work. I needed the money to use for acting expenses. During those times, I was not in treatment, and I would spend my time working, dealing with people and attempting jobs as an actor. I found that my income was low, always, and I never really got on my feet, as my bills would always bring me down. I never found a way out of low income; I was doing ok, but I needed to do something to pursue my career. Seeing a psychologist or a psychiatrist wasn't a part of my plan.

I was happy enough to stay out of the doctor's office as I spent time working or acting, or fundraising, for that matter, as a job. I had to live my life whether it meant living it in Colorado or the big city streets of New York. I held numerous jobs during this time and tried to find something that I could do to make some money, but it seemed difficult. I worked at fast food, I worked at a bank and I worked at a restaurant. I found that the corporations were looking for perfection and I didn't fit. The struggle seemed to be as big as ever because I couldn't keep the jobs that I wanted, and I wasn't really even sure what I was doing anything for. I wasn't acting, I wasn't doing anything really productive and I was having problems with the people that had hired me. I had always had to look out for myself, and working two jobs and traveling to and from each job was not working. Looking back, I feel that there was more involved with just getting to the job and spending money on gas and transportation and insurance, all just to make it to work, and it was counterproductive if I wanted to actually make any money working. I really never had control during this time.

This is My Playground

In 2010 I decided to move to New York
to find a job and get back into acting. I
decided to go east this time, to be in the city,
among the buildings and to find a life. I had a
friend there at that time let me stay with her
for a short period and then I found a place to
live in a dirty borough of Brooklyn. During this
time I wasn't seeing a psychologist or a
psychiatrist for anything. I spent two years in
New York working for a fundraising company
for arts organizations and non profits. It was a
good experience, but I found that it was all I
could find, while I was out there, and really
nothing existed to make a solid living off of. I
find even to this day, that being out of work as
an actor, is really non-productive, but I have
lost the drive to try any more as no one has the
ability to pay anything but the larger networks
on television and in film. That is where the

money is. I knew myself enough that I didn't need to make appointments with a psychologist out in New York, and I didn't make any attempt to. I found it almost counter productive. The more time I spent on a psychiatrists couch, the less time I was spending finding work or doing what I wanted to while I was there.

While in New York, I found jobs as an actor on television and in film. I hadn't really worked as an actor since 2003, when I left California. It just shows you that if you want a part of the entertainment industry, you need to move to one of the coasts in the United States. Everything is in those cities. However, moving to New York, as talked about earlier, I found myself living in "affordable" housing and in a situation where the money I earned working was spent for rent; I found this counterproductive in saving anything I made for the future. Anything I made for work would go to pay bills, and to have a place to sleep at night. I know that seems normal, and probably a lot of the nation works in that regard. However, I found myself sleeping in a place that wasn't a place that I could call my own and a place where I could call home. I didn't like the fact that my money went to a place that had squirrels in the attic and rats in the basement. This was just some of what I had to deal with while living there and I couldn't afford anything better.

What I enjoyed about life in New York was the chance to be myself and do what I could to survive. I will say that finding work as an actor was difficult regardless, but it helped that the major companies and work was available to me there. I knew how to act; I had done it for much of my younger days in and out of college and in California. It was nice to be back into it. I have always been involved in the arts somehow and creating things was important to me. New York gave me an opportunity to work again and live the way I wanted. I had to, of course, deal with the issues of everyone around me; as an actor you are thrown amidst a lot of controversy and many different people trying to survive and make it. It was nice, unless of course I got tired of it, which would happen.

I have come to realize that in life, I want to make it known that this is my playground. In my life so far, I can say that if I truly want to do something, I have done it, and at least tried to make it successful. I have had problems along the way, and getting psychological and mental help has given me more freedom. By getting the help I needed through the times I have, it has helped me see which freedoms are important to me as a person, and given me room to grow. While I was in New York, I was on television and in film, something that was legitimate and willful employment. I was genuinely happy to be there and I am happy I took the risk to move there when I did. I tell myself that now, if I do go back to pursue the career in the future that I will move out to California again. I don't think I will ever go back to New York for a number or reasons, primarily economic.

I chose a career, that, unless you are cast in a large play or a television program, or a film, it is pretty difficult to make any money. Even working as an actor in New York on television, for the time I was there, I really only made a day wage that was low and barely made me any money. It is unfortunate, but money makes the world go around, and if I am the one who doesn't have it, I try to be the one that gets it. Working as an extra on television shows was a start, but living in the slums of Brooklyn, was probably the worst living situation I had to go through. While I was there I had to rent a room, which was small and didn't have adequate space. It had bugs, squirrels, like I said, and also rats in the basement. If I further my career as an actor in the future, you won't find me living in a place where there are living conditions such as those. If living conditions contribute to a person's mental health, this place I lived was surely a factor which I don't want to deal with ever again.

Throughout my life thus far I have dealt with issues and problems that came from either a difficult career choice to problems of failing infrastructure. Because I have had a low wage as an actor, I have had to struggle more often than if I was in a different profession. I have had to work part time jobs and I have had to try to survive. If I had chosen a different career path, and there is still time to go back to school, and I had given thought to pursue my life as a dentist for example, I suppose my financial situation would be different, and thus my mental health could possibly change. I have noticed that I have had difficult mental problems, and I believe that the reason is due to the lack of money and the ability to survive under such conditions. If I were to go back to school for another career choice I could possibly have the ability to get out of poverty and make something more of myself, and not have to move to a large city to be successful.

In fact, I have given some thought to a different career in the recent past living in Colorado. I have grown to understand that my career as an actor could be short lived. Living in this state, I have found that many of the issues I come to experience are because of the fact that I am on a fixed income with no leeway to do the things that I may desire to do, one of which would be to get married or to have a family, or to even buy a house for myself. Because housing costs rise each year and if you are not making a decent salary, then it comes down to not being able to afford what you have. I have noticed that most of my adult professional life I have been trying to afford something, rather than simply affording it. I hope that makes sense. There are those who can afford a new car without the old one breaking, and can afford a home at a high price, because of their salary. I have low income status and because of this I am always on a strict budget, and I am usually alone when it comes to making decisions. An option I am going to keep open is to work toward a sort of sub-career as a writer and bring to light the issues I have had in my life thus far. Thankfully they aren't as serious as some would say, but to me they have been very pertinent.

The playground is for sharing and that is just what I intend to do. As a child I shared the playground with others in their backgrounds. I spent time on the monkey bars as a kid climbing away. I just want to make sure that when my day comes, that I have learned to play well with others, as many people set out to do, but don't realize how important that it can be. If you see another person coming down the monkey bars the opposite direction, be sure to yield for them so that there doesn't become a problem for both of you. I have learned, through much of my life and career thus far, that playing well with others is important, as we all have to live here collectively, and mental health can be a major player in understanding it all.

Anger and Reasoning

Getting angry about things has been what I would call a strong suit, in my twenties. I found myself getting angry at a number of things that seemed out of my control and I would find myself arguing with loved ones and becoming angry at situations that I didn't like. I had a lot of anger issues as a child too. I didn't want to get into trouble, and I found that arguing made me feel better, but wouldn't fix everything. I was overwhelmed at times as a child and even into my teenage years as I was presented with things that again were out of my control. Something like a school schedule, or a class that I didn't want to attend, or maybe even wearing an article of clothing that I wasn't happy with made me feel constricted and not happy. Also, as a child I would find myself getting angry things that I didn't like or I had to do. Going to school, was

something I didn't necessarily enjoy to begin
with; I would rather stay by myself than go off
with a big group of people where I was forced
to act or react, and didn't always get along
with them. Those things I didn't enjoy one bit.
When I was forced to be nice or be polite, I
began to realize that I was in fact a bit
uncaring, as any child can be.

I suppose what I remember as a young
person was a number of people that were
uncaring and sometimes harsh to my learning
process and my ability to be honest and
upfront. I think I needed more than most as a
child, but I was surrounded by people that
came from all walks of life and because of this I
developed a sense of the world that came
before me, and was old. I learned to be myself
as most do through trial and error and from
simply doing things on my own. I would get
angry when I didn't get what I wanted or
things didn't go my way. These days, when I

sense things are not going my way, I find myself wanting to change them. I try and do things differently or try and find a way to get a better view. I don't get as angry as I used to; I use my reasoning. I don't know if being on medication now has anything to do with that, but I have noticed that a lot of what I get angry at, can be avoided these days, however there are times that I simply can't control the change that is occurring in my life on a daily basis. I attempt to control it, but sometimes I have to let it go.

I have been known to angry at people for not doing their job correctly, or when I come to expect something of a person or a place, and they do not deliver what I have come to think, then I find myself getting angry. When I deal with the products that people produce, and of course I use a variety of other people's things everyday, as I don't have a company that produces things, I end up spending my money on other people's products, and this makes me angry. When I am writing a paper and I get a large amount of noise from outside that I can't control, this makes me angry sometimes. I do what I can to control the things in my life, but sometimes it seems that they have been out of control for a good part of my life, especially when I have attempted to work for places that create all of these rules that they put into place for people to follow. I have had difficulty working for places that instill so many rules.

What also gets me angry is disorganization. I can't control the world's differences, as I find that different people organize different ways. For example when I visit my parent's house on the weekends I look at their bookshelf and find that their organization is by subject, not by author. In my apartment I have my books organized by author. I have done this as I have found that I like things in alphabetical order. It bothers me when I see things out of order, and I would like to have them organized. I suppose this gives me a reason to be angry, as it also something that I can't control. When I got my library back after being gone for a few years, in New York, I found myself organizing my books, because I needed to be doing something productive. Leaving a large city, I found my skills had improved to do things in general. For example, I noticed my cleaning skills were better after having lived in a dirty rotten apartment in Brooklyn, NY. I found that I was able to clean at a faster rate, and I understood that picking up for me was important. I realized that no one would do it for me, and I had to be the one to be responsible for everything.

Some of the large part of responsibility came from realizing that no one would do anything for me, and I had to make sure it got done. It was pretty bad actually when I lived in a large city. Yes, the freedom was there, but I found myself having to do a lot, just to keep myself running. For example, shopping for groceries, and also cleaning things that I had to, to make sure things were sanitary. Some of these basic chores and errands were fine, and didn't make me angry, but I found myself getting angry when I did my part in life and many of the people around me didn't. So, thankfully I have learned a little more about other people and their ways of life, versus mine, where I try and keep things clean and livable. I would get angry when I couldn't control what other people did.

As I have lived in different places, I have found that different people live different ways. I don't know for sure what I should expect from everyone, but my reasoning says that it is still hard to trust people you don't know. My reasoning is that "these" people can't be trusted, or watch out who you trust, and it has become harder to find people who are trustworthy in life. It is sad, when you go through life feeling that there is not a person who cane be trusted, or would care enough to trust me in life. I hope that changes sometime, but wherever I have moved, infrastructure has been run down, and under maintained. When I have had to do things that are unnecessarily out of my way in life, I find that I don't want to do these things, if it all goes to benefit someone else. I don't find myself enjoying those actions. When it all comes down to it, I feel that it all goes to benefit someone else.

These are just some of the things that make me angry, and surely I could go on, for example, when one works all month and then the landlord takes the money and what I have found is at the end of the week, it doesn't make me feel very good. Then I see the trash overflowing with McDonald's bags. I ask myself is that where my money is going? I suppose that is something that makes me angry. I don't expect a free ride, although going through my twenties and now thirties it is just becoming more obvious to me that there will never be anyone that I can lean on, or rely on, as it is all just me. I find that a good friend doesn't make me angry, especially when there is one that can cheer me up with a little laughter, but if a friendship is all politics, and then there is really no point. I suppose the mail system makes me angry too. It's usually due to the fact that if I didn't take care of it all myself, they would just bring me bills, wherever I am. This week, on Tuesday I got coupons from local places in town that I can go eat. Money is another reason to be angry as I don't have a lot of it, and I can basically pay my bills with my disability money, but I find that it doesn't go any further than that. The use of money can make me angry, although I try and find ways to use it to make life more enjoyable.

These are my reasons for being angry. I suppose when I get down to the fact that at the end of the day, no one is there, and won't be later in life; I find the world to be an angry place. I guess I need to get out more.

The Daily Life of Me

After moving back to Colorado following a two year working trip to New York, I find that my daily activities change regularly, but recently have been becoming stagnant. A week goes by and I usually try to accomplish a number of things, and recently I have been writing songs, poetry and political books and now this, a paper dedicated to the mental health of my life. Currently I live out of my one bedroom apartment in Colorado Springs, Colorado, where I usually get to enjoy the weather and the sunshine that God brings daily, and helps me understand why there are seven days in a week. I sleep a lot and try and feed myself, and even exercise. My daily life is usually spent alone with my new dog Buster.

I wake up at somewhere between five and six a.m. and take him out to relieve himself. Then, what I have been doing since the beginning of the year of 2016 is going back to bed for a couple of hours and then getting up around eight a.m., to begin my day. I will then take Buster out again and come back in to make myself some breakfast. Today was an egg omelet scramble sort of thing with some ham and tomato. Then I had some juice and an orange. There is only so much to do since I am on food stamps and have very low income. So, I will make some breakfast, and I shop normally at the beginning of the week which allows me to stay put for most of the week and not have to run out of food. After breakfast, lately I have been getting a notebook together or opening up my computer, a small laptop that is now about seven years old, to work on my books or short stories. I have even been transcribing from the notebook I have, where I will sit and write something first and then afterward write it into the computer so I can make a file out of it or a selection of poems or stories into a book. I have used the internet to become more productive, I have been making a couple books through a website and have done some self publishing. It has kept me out of all the eyes of the major publishers who analyze every detail to see if something is marketable.

I have been skipping lunch lately and I only have two meals a day because the medication I have been taking has made me gain some weight. Living in this apartment I have become lazier and have slept more, and I don't know if it might be a side effect, but I have gained weight living here, which doesn't make any sense because I live in the mountains where there is hiking and all sorts of outdoor activities. I spend a lot of time inside, and find that being outside hiking all the time doesn't do much for one's productivity. Personally I have found ways to be productive without spending a lot of money. For example I have bought a notepad and written, filling up the pages with journal entries, ideas and poems, short stories and movie script ideas. I also have bought a sketch pad that allows me to draw and color things that I might think of, and then I will, using my computer, upload them to have a digital file made for viewing or sharing through the internet to family members.

I try to see friends. I have a few people I know in Colorado, and I have been able to spend time with them while being here. I left a long time ago to live in another city, to work, to go to school and such. However, now, many of my previous friends have all gotten married o̶r̶ and had some children, which is fine, but I have never come across a woman that I thought would have my children, so I guess that is the way it will be or at least has been for some time now. During the day I have been writing, or spending a lot of time being creative. For example, writing a poem, three pages of something that I can say at the end of the day that I have done something with it, is that which I can call me. I don't know if it is worth anything, but I feel good after the day is done, because I can say I have at least accomplished something. Since I am living off a very low income, I have found that spending my day doing something creative, and not sitting and drinking my day away at a local bar or doing something that ultimately costs money, are the things I enjoy doing, because I can say I have been productive, and not just a lazy bum.

I cook. I can say that I don't go out to eat a lot. I have been taught by the best, my mother. I will say that on any given day of the week, I am cooking and finding something in the pantry or refrigerator to eat, and I usually try and grocery shop once per week. If I spend my time going out, I spend money that I don't have, and I find it to be a very fun experience.

I think there is a chance that I find a place every now and then that I would enjoy to eat at, however I don't usually want to spend the money going out. I don't really like eating among other people's families. I have found that in the past, and I will get into this more later, that many families are dirty and have terrible eating habits, that I of course notice, having been on my own for a fair amount of time. I have really never had a good time going out to eat, because I have found that other people's families are not clean and have a bunch of issues that I would rather not get involved in. So, I choose to cook and work from home and stay out of all of it. I mean, it's not like I just don't go out to eat, but after being diagnosed, I really found myself more focused on myself and getting healthy, and going to a fast food restaurant or a large American dining restaurant really didn't help things.

I watch television sometimes. In and out of my daily creation of the writings I have been working on, I have found that writing is really something that I can do, and enjoy doing, and doesn't require me to go out, drive, and pay for everything that people want you to pay for their survival. I am looking out for myself, and I can honestly say that there have been problems when I try to go out and get involved in other people's activities. So, I choose to watch some television each day to see what is going on out there. I listen to the radio to get an update on news and weather. I know I am not alone when it comes to doing these things, and I think there are people that can say they watch a fair amount of television or listen to the radio. I watch shows like courtroom dramas, a couple of situation comedies and some sports. I have had the same television for nearly seventeen years and when I moved it all went into storage. But I have found that having a television can be a great way to get information about one's safety, and if I lived anywhere else, I would have to rely on some news source to make sure I was safe.

The radio, books and magazines find their way into my life lately. I try and read a variety of different news sources and also I was given a few different free subscriptions to magazines that I can read to get news from other places. I choose to live where I do because I am close to my family and I am far away from all the problems of other people, and I am happy to wake up and see the mountains. I used to live where I would wake up and see buildings and it was a bit difficult to enjoy life when one knew that their rent payment was to pay for fixing all the problems in the building.

In January, 2016, I rescued a dog from the Humane Society in my city and I spend time with him everyday. I find him to be helpful to help my quality of life, and when there is a dull moment, I have something to do. I will take the dog out to spend time with him outside for a little while. The days get dark fast in the winter where I live and days and nights come and go swiftly. My dog is named Buster, and he is a smooth haired fox terrier mix. I did some research and it is an English breed that has some nice looking colors like black brown and white markings. I feed him twice a day and it gives me something to live for when I don't have anything else. I have given myself some things to do, like write a couple different books and make some different projects for myself to pass the time and keep me busy. When I was younger I always had something to do, and found ways to pass the time by playing games, putting a model car together, painting, listening to music and playing with toys or writing or coloring.

I have a place to live that allows pets, and if I lived in a house, I wouldn't be able to afford it, because my income is so low. I have been forced into renting because the housing market is so expensive. I also enjoy listening to music and researching different types of books and authors, and if I have a goal to do something I find myself researching them first before I make an attempt to do make something of my own. For example, my recent book, "The Poetry of D. L. Arber, I used what I learned from different poets who I had in my home library. I went back over the books and eventually found my voice in writing, and soon came to have a lot of work that I put together in a collection.

This past summer I gardened. I found a productive way to get outside, and my mother gave me some planters that I could fill with mulch and plant flowers and food for consumption. As it got warmer and the spring turned to summer, I spent time filling the planters. I would go to the nursery to get plants to put out on my patio. This year I got a tomato plant, and I planted lettuce, spinach, radishes, and then, living in the state of Colorado, I even planted a marijuana plant. I had to get rid of it because there was a term in my apartment lease that stated I could not have marijuana on the grounds. If I ever get a house in the future, I will probably grow it for fun. I did think about smoking it, but I never did, for a few reasons. One is because I think there would be some psychoactive ingredients in the pot that would not mix well with my current medication. The other reason is smoking pot is another way to get into trouble, and when I was younger I was prone to having something happen, or getting into trouble somehow.

These are just some of the things I do to spend my days lately. After being diagnosed, I have tried to find ways to expand my mental awareness and physical health without spending my money. I stay active and out of trouble, and on the positive side of things. I am thankful I have a couple close friends that I can see from time to time who I can have discussions with about life, work, and God. On the downside of things, I am still working from home and some days I do feel alone. So, I think there is a time and place for being by one's self, and then a time for being with friends and family. As far as the new addition to my life this year, it is a dog. He has been good to me so far.

Secrets and Life

I would first say that a lot of my life I have had my secrets. However, I haven't had enough to really hold on to or that would give me clout if I were to disclose them in a board room among officials. I find that I have had my own holdings in a number of areas only because I have not needed to be open about things in certain circumstances. I am choosing to write this book only because I hope in doing so it will make me more aware of myself and my life. I am happy that I have the ability to hold back in a number of situations and obviously I have learned that many times in life it is not good to disclose one's secrets, because they can be used against you in a number of situations. I choose to remain quiet. I don't in reality have secrets that I hold to myself and choose not to tell; it's just that I don't really have anyone to tell them to, and that may be for the best.

I have found that being diagnosed with schizophrenia brings with it some paranoia that wouldn't normally be there. I have noticed that if I have a conversation with someone, I am usually afraid that if I say too much about myself, that people will judge me or believe I am not as much of a human being. If I choose to tell them I have a disability, I would think that the first thing they will think will be that he is not as fit a human being as the next guy, and that I will be put to the side. I have found that in real life, not many people can be trusted with these types of information, and I am not really willing to provide these things to just anyone off the street.

I have friends for the reason that I can give them the information about myself that I wouldn't give to just anyone; and I have been aware that what I tell them stays between them and me and no one else. My friends are close and I wouldn't want to jeopardize information I say about me to be revealed to others; I want it to be kept safe. I would say that if I had to make a will because I was getting older and had no one, and no beneficiaries, then I would have to come up with someone, like a close friend or family member, if I had one, to give my things to when I die. This type of information would be shared among the people I choose. I find that in life, I only want to share important information with those that I love and cherish. My close friends and family are the ones that I want to know things about me, not just someone I meet at a grocery or at a shopping mall.

I don't have really many secrets to disclose, however, I have found that before I was on medication, I would feel that everyone was on my back trying to figure out these things about me and were quite a bit nosey. I find that is the case with people in general; they want to know about things, and when they do, they find out what they want and then turn away. Once they find out what they came for, then they make a decision about whether or not they want to continue to get to know you. I find this disheartening. Throughout my twenties, and into my thirties I have grown to distrust many people as I have found that they aren't really ever there for the right reasons, but where I live people seem to be nice, but really are only pleasant because they are getting paid. If they weren't paid, then there is a chance that they wouldn't be nice or fair; I think they would be just like everyone else, greedy and nosey.

Again, I say that I don't have much to hide, but when I want my privacy, I want my space. I am not looking for people to try and get in my way and cause trouble. I find it interesting that many people find ways to get your time and money, and when I want my space, it is hard to find space that doesn't cost. It is an unfortunate event, but when I want my space, it is not because I have secrets to hide from others; it is just a basic need for privacy, not secrecy.

I find that fewer people lead to fewer issues along the spectrum of privacy and secrecy. It is like the game of telephone. I played this as a child. School children line up in a row and then express a word or a phrase at one end of the line and then speak it to the next child in line until it reaches the other end. By the time the child at the end of the line receives the word or phrase, they have it all jumbled around and mixed up! For example, if my word or phrase that I begin with is, "I have ten fingers and ten toes," and each child speaks the phrase to the next, then what comes out at the end could be, "Time lingers on the child's nose!" Not that it would be that, but my point is that it could be that as I see it and such is the case in life! Many people take what you tell them and blow it out of proportion. This is why I keep anything I can, a secret.

I have found that after my diagnosis, secrets are also left for those that are helping me medically or mentally. This means that anything that I have come up with, I don't usually share with just anyone, but will talk these things over with my psychologist and psychiatrist. When the time comes to see my psychiatrist again, I will speak with them about pertinent information about me, or things that have come up during the last few weeks and relay to them what I believe could be worked on or changed. I usually hold these things in and then let them know if I have anything that I haven't told anyone, and then I usually disclose it in our meetings. Things that make me angry aren't really secrets; I am usually aware of these things, but normally keep them to myself. I feel that keeping things to myself aren't really secrets, but are points that I don't want to share with just anyone.

In my past, I have lived. I suppose up until this day I have been involved in a number of activities, in career choices and in life events. I would say that I spend a lot of time by myself and always have only because I am an only child to begin with; that is no secret, and it lends itself to being alone. I haven't really met anyone else that wants to help me get out of being alone; it just sort of comes with what I do, and what I am. For example, the places I have traveled, where I have gone to school, and friends I know aren't really secrets, but are just information about me that someone could find out about me if they simply asked me, but normally I don't get asked.

Anything that I find to be an important part of life and something that I would only want to stay within the family or close friends, I don't really speak about to any person in my life. I find myself holding on to that information as these people don't really know anything about you. I think there is a chance that they could take that information and abuse it, and for this reason I choose to remain private. In the future that may change, but as of today, I like to keep to myself and continue to unless asked for these sorts of things. As far as family is concerned, these are the people that know nearly everything about me and it will continue to stay this way. I just hope there is someone that I can meet in the near future that I can make an addition to my family, so I may begin to share things with them, and not be sworn to secrecy.

Food and Drink

I can imagine all the things I love to eat.
I also can find the time to devour a lovely
piece of food. I suppose I am among the new
generations foodie culture where I like to
indulge in sweet meals and tasty treats. I must
let you know that on a fixed budget it can be
difficult. In fact, when you are rationed to a
low $194 per month when purchasing food it
goes to show you how much one can buy and
one can afford. Food costs a pretty penny, but
I can usually find some inexpensive items.
When it comes down to food and drink, there
are some things I try to stay away from and
also try to meet a requirement of each week.
One thing that has remained constant all my
life is that I have had to purchase food and
drink each and almost every week. Whether I
am working or not, I can tell you that it is
important to eat.

I know what you are asking, but of course eating healthy meals has a lot to do with mental health. Before my diagnosis, I didn't give as much thought to it as I do, but being alone all the time, I find myself eating things from cans, packaged meals, and frozen dinners. As I discussed before I don't go out to eat and spend my money on restaurants, because I find that it all seems to go into someone else's pocket. I find that I have to be aware of what I spend and where it all goes. I have been more aware of this as I have less to spend. I am by no means a millionaire, and living on a fixed income only pressures me in certain ways and makes it difficult to even eat healthy. In my opinion, the system should change, but I can be thankful that I at least get a little help to buy food each month.

I like food like steak, fish and chicken. My favorite food is still lasagna. There are a few reasons for that actually (and this actually could be one of my secrets), but I will tell you it is because the comic cat Garfield loves lasagna, and I have loved Garfield since I was a young person. I like pizza and I enjoy pasta. Lately I have been buying a frozen cheese pizza from the supermarket and putting my own toppings on it. The toppings I choose are mushrooms and anchovies. Some of you out there are probably thinking that is gross, but others are maybe thinking I am adventurous! Anyway, I will put some toppings on a store bought pizza instead of order out for pizza delivery.

Another food I like is oysters. I like things that are healthy and tasty. I don't get to eat oysters but very rarely, like once a year, but when I do, I enjoy them. I think there is also room for seafood in my diet. I like deli food too, of course being on public assistance, I don't go out to eat but once a month or less. I simply can't afford it. But it is important that I eat healthy, so I make things each night that

are good for you. For example, with a soup
and sandwich I will make a salad. In the salad
I will put lettuce, tomatoes, avocado and then
sometimes some olives and then even some
artichoke hearts. Then I will put some store
bought salad dressing on it, and recently I have
even been using organic mayonnaise and put
a spoonful on the salad when I run out of
normal dressing. Some things I switch around,
and try new things as I see them on television
cooking shows but some things I figure out for
myself. For example, I put anchovies on a
pizza that is store bought and divide them all
over the pizza and I find it pleasing. Once a
week I will have pizza if possible and I even
have put on slices of tomatoes to make it tasty
and a healthier option.

I describe how I make some things and
the options I have because I have found that if
one doesn't express themselves through
cooking, or eating, that it becomes a dull,

boring life. Some people don't think that eating is important, but I am here to tell you that it is. In all the things that become corrupt when you become diagnosed with an illness that is supposed to be incurable, and the stigma and problem it becomes when meeting anyone, I find that my creativity in life lends itself to making the illness more manageable.

Something else that I found interesting is that people with schizophrenia are prone to alcoholism. I found in my classes at the National Alliance for Mental Illness, that alcohol was a driving factor in those people that had a mental illness. Also, smoking was a factor in those that had an illness. I used to smoke when I was younger, and when I was in my twenties, I would drink from time to time while on my travels and in college. I have recently stopped drinking since moving home to Colorado again in 2013. I have felt that it really has been a reason for being unproductive. It is also a reason to kill a lot of time, and it feels like I really don't have a lot of time to spend drinking and socializing. I have realized since I have been diagnosed that I only have a set number of days on the planet and I try to be productive everyday and stay out of a destructive environment.

I have been brought up in a household that doesn't drink regularly, but will have a glass of wine or a beer every so often on holidays or birthdays. You will not find me buying beer from the local liquor store because for one, I am on a fixed income and two, I just don't want to be drinking alone, and I find myself being alone a lot of the time. Now, I know the consequences of drinking, and I have chosen not to because it is important to try and drink healthier options like apple juice, or cranberry juice, or even seltzer water which has some fizzing bubbles that sooth the senses.

When it comes to food and drink, like many of the other things in my life, I try to get creative with my options, I suppose, because I could drink water, and that is always an option, because I live in America, and I have running tap water that is clean and fresh. I really shouldn't take that for granted, but when I have a chance to try a new juice, or a new drink of some kind, then I do take that option. When food is presented to me, I never turn down a good meal from a family member or friend or neighbor, and when I can make something that I enjoy, I try and do it, because it keeps me thinking of something different; this is why there are so many options at the grocery; it keeps one coming back to try something different the next week of shopping. Food and drink have an effect on a person's overall mental health.

People and Cleanliness

I confess; I am aware of a person's hygiene. I didn't become aware of the word hygiene until I began speaking with my mental health professional. We began by talking about routine and the different things I do each day to make sure I stay a healthy and happy adult. I have been in a number of places that seem to be pleasing to the eye on the outside, but when entering the establishment, find that the place is dirty, unclean and unsanitary. I have since stopped going out to a number of places in town regularly and taking care of things as I see fit on my end where I live and stay. However, these places exist. Along with people, there are simple cleanliness characteristics that people and places have and should be brought to light. There are a number of things I make sure I do, and have done since I was a young person that contribute to my mental health and I it is true that personal hygiene has an effect on how a person views others, and also how others view you.

First, let's start with one's self. Skin, teeth and hair are the main topics that people with poor mental health should pay attention to. All my life, I have brushed my hair thousands of times most likely, and I have brushed my teeth thousands of times. When I was diagnosed with schizophrenia, I noticed that I really wasn't paying as much attention to these things, but when I was made aware of them again; I realized how important they are. Brushing one's teeth is a basic action that people miss sometimes, and those that have serious health issues usually have bad teeth because they are neglecting themselves in that area. I have been taught that hair is a protein and so are nails. These are things that I don't pay much attention to but when it was brought to light, I began to start to take better care of myself, and be aware of how fast my fingernails would grow or watch just how long my hair would grow between haircuts. These are things I didn't pay that much attention to when I was younger, but I always wanted a nice haircut. I even paid more than I needed to get it trimmed and styled.

I have always made sure that when I clean things on myself, I am thorough, and I like to make sure I am clean inside and out. That is why, with an illness, I sort of think of the medication as cleaning my mind in a way, so that I can think clearly again. When I rode the subway system in New York, there were people of all walks of life taking the trains, and it most likely took a team of people to keep the trains clean. I felt that of the people I saw everyday, some would take care of themselves and others didn't, or couldn't. I realized how important my normal everyday activities or routine began to mean so much after seeing other people's way of life and how some live, especially the ones that were in poverty or had low income like me. I felt that these people didn't take care of themselves as I did, and I felt that their hygiene was lacking. This was my view, but even then before I got any mental help, I noticed these things in people, and really just thought as I grew up that people were dirtier than I was as you may notice in your own life, if you live around a certain type of people for some time, you will begin to act similarly. I noticed myself while I lived in different places and met different people, that I would sort of assimilate to the people I was around to sort of get along.

What I don't take for granted now, that I live in a cleaner area and out of the terrible poverty that I used to live in, is that I value the use of a shower. After seeing a healthcare professional, I sort of began to realize that it is all in one package when dealing with a person, and that most days when I can and have the time, make sure I wash myself at least once a day. Taking a shower once a day may not seem important, but if everyone showered at least once a day, the world would be a lot more sanitary and the use of things like lotions and colognes and sanitizers would go down.

Different cultures have different ways of being sanitary and clean. I have noticed living in different cities that different people take care of themselves differently. The Chinese man probably cleans himself differently than an African woman, and the English man who bathes in a bathtub is different than the construction worker that uses the shower to get all the dirt and grime off at the end of a day. The Japanese woman who bathes in red flower petals obviously cleans herself differently than that of a migrant farmer who has worked all day in the fields. My point being, as an artist, actor and writer, I have noticed that grime and dust=accumulates on my nose and body after a day at the computer, taking my dog out or just running errands. At the end of the day, I want to clean up.

Since I have lived on my own for such a long time, I have noticed that when I get around others, their ways of life are much different than mine and I find that cleanliness is not as valued as I now value it. When I simply walk outside of where I currently live, I have noticed that there are just simple differences that make me aware of hygiene and how people take care of themselves; unlike me, I don't believe they value hygiene and cleanliness as I now do.

Basic hygiene is different than getting dirty. Working as a construction worker, you will get dirty. If you are homeless, you are probably dirty. If you are a cook and deal with food all day, I hope that when and if I have to go to your restaurant (although I normally stay in now), but if I had to be served by you, that you would hopefully be sanitary and clean. I make sure that I clean myself and so should you. I find that people with mental illness (at least the ones I run into) are aware of these things after they have gotten help, whereas before, the ones I have come into contact with are not the cleanest of people. Not to judge, but there is definitely a difference from someone who understands what a shower is and does and someone who doesn't. I have become more aware of what a clean body and a clean mind feels like, and I can tell you that when you have mental help from a professional, they will help you clean up your life, if you desire.

I have found that the dirtier people have less care for others. If you walk into a bus, or get on a subway train someplace, the cleaner people are not looking out for themselves, but are concerned how the world views them more than dirtier people. I think that means they care more about themselves and others. The people that are dirtier and don't have much care for personal hygiene are really uncaring people about others around them. It is just an observation. It just seems that when I meet people from other countries, and of other walks of life, I have found that a lot of them don't concern themselves with hygiene; I think this could in fact inadvertently be a mental health issue.

The fact is, no one wants to be around someone who is filthy while they eat, sleep or work, which is the reason that I choose to stay in and cook. Don't get me wrong. On the weekend I get out, and go outside and breathe the fresh air of Colorado, where I currently live; however, I don't find myself frequenting places that have all the filthy workers and unclean working environments. So, that said, I find that in mental health, cleanliness and personal hygiene remains an integral part of one's ability to be a functioning and working individual. I find it to be very important, as getting back into the swing of things in life and getting one's personal life grounded and back on track. Simplicity is key and keeping clean without the use of odors and scents; those that use colognes to keep clean are just masking the things that are dirty.

Safety and Living

I have found that there are a number
of things that I take into account when finding
a place to live. Whenever I've lived
somewhere I've taken into account the safety
of the neighborhood, the safety of myself, the
safety of the people I am living nearby. In the
future, I will try to search for the crime rate in
the neighborhood that I will be living in, if it is
available. The first place I got on my own in
California was an interesting place. It was a
duplex, where there were four apartments;
two on the first floor and two on the second
floor. The apartments themselves weren't the
problem; it was the people in the area that
turned out to be the issue. There was a local
convenience store just like in most
neighborhoods with a gas station attached just
down the block on the corner. Then there was

a park, and you had to cross a highway bridge to get over and walk through to it.

Of all the places I've lived, I have begun to notice what is safe and what is not safe about the place I live, as time goes on. For example, when I lived in New York City the first time, I lived in Chinatown and had a three floor walk-up that had a building with two doors for entry and a fire escape that was above ground and would only extend to the ground if there was someone on it. However, the second time I lived in New York I lived in the borough of Brooklyn where the only place I could find was a house that was converted into three apartments inside with a shared living space. When I lived in one of those apartments, there was a lock on the door at the basement to enter the building, and then there were three separate doors to each apartment that also had a lock. Tenants were given keys to all the doors in the building.

When I lived in Chinatown, I suppose there was the normal everyday crime in the neighborhood, but in fact it was a fairly safe place for whatever reason.

The time I lived in Brooklyn, was the first time I had to file a police report on the tenant above me for stealing my keys to my entrance and the apartment door dedicated to my living space. It was the first time I was robbed in my life. There were locks on the door, but I believe what happened and I can't recall completely, but I believe I was using the restroom when the upstairs tenant reached in and stole my keys. Little did I know that the landlord had rented to a person who had a previous criminal history. What I had to do is file a police report and complaint against the tenant and call the landlord to get new keys issued to me. It was not a fun time in my life and ultimately would probably determine a decision I would make to leave New York and come back to Colorado, to where I grew up.

I found that safety in a living space is very important to me, and I learned from experience that safety is one thing I must look for when renting a space and looking out for my personal belongings in my life. I have found again, that people are not to be trusted, at least certain people and I have really never been around much better. When I moved back to Colorado and into the current building where I live, I found that the first couple of months were when I began to get things set up to live here. I was on the fifth floor of the building which had fifty units and a number of residents. There is a community room in the building and I got to know an old man who had lived in the building for a number of years. In fact, the building had a number of older residents, whereas in the previous tenancies I lived among people closer in age. So, I began speaking with the old man regularly and I got to know him and we would sit in the community room and talk about where we both came from to end up here.

In the community room were a few cushion chairs, a refrigerator, and a laundry machine where you could load a laundry card up with money, and then there was a television. It worked when I moved here, but after time, it stopped working and would have its problems. Regardless, there were windows in the community room that really were not secure, and one night or early morning, sure enough, here came some robbers to steal the television. It happened overnight and in the morning, the residents were left with a blank wall and no entertainment. There were even locks on the doors to the leasing office and the front door of the building, but when the criminals came to steal the television, they took it through the window in the community room.

I am not sure if this is true, and how all of this comes to have much to do with mental illness, but I have this belief that there are people in the world whose sole purpose in life is to destroy the happiness of the elderly and disabled and those less fortunate. It's just a hunch, but I have felt this way when I look into the eyes of criminals on the nightly news. I don't think this has anything to do with mental health, but in a roundabout way it does, because I feel it is a right of every resident who is looking for a safe place to live, that they should be able to find a place that is safe, clean and honest. I have found that having to live in places that are low income based, or have lower rents, a resident is prone to crime in a way, I am not happy with.

Since that occurrence, not much comes to mind when it comes to crime in my recent past. I live a pretty quiet life and I do my best to stay out of trouble, however in the past it seems to have found me. When there is money around, I find that people are looking for it, and for a reason to create crime. I am just happy I have found a place where the crime rate is fairly low, but I can tell you that living in apartments over time, I have just grown to expect a fair amount of delinquency. I suppose it also comes with the city and where one actually resides. I have found that keeping to myself has its benefits only because there are people in life that only live to take advantage of others. Mentally, these things play a role for me, and I have felt relieved that I survived the previous problems in New York, California, and briefly in Colorado. I have found that there is crime everywhere and that my awareness of being mentally disabled has helped me survive in times that are unsure and unclear.

I only hope that I will continue to be safe in my actions and to live in a safe area that is a bit predictable. I would rather live a bit of a predictable life currently than an abrupt, chaotic and dangerous one. Having schizophrenia, I need a place that is quiet, calm and safe to live. It is hard enough to be on top of other people in the apartment building where I live, let alone being able to find a place to work. Being around other people doesn't pose a threat to me; it is just getting along with the occasional gossip.

Relationships

In my life to date I have had a few important relationships. During my youth I found time to meet girls in a variety of different ways. I would meet some girls at school and then I would meet some outside of school in my neighborhood. When I got my first job at 15 I met someone there too. Girls have come and gone and I have had a variety of relationships throughout my life. Not only girls, but important relationships like family and community involvement as well as teachers and coworkers have played a role throughout my life so far. Over the course of thirty eight years I have had a variety of relationships that have contributed to my individual learning as an adult.

Having a mental illness, or at least as I see it, being diagnosed as a mentally ill adult, I have found that it becomes more and more difficult to have lasting meaningful relationships with people. I have found that there comes a more and more difficult problem of meeting people when everyone is out there for themselves anyway. Over the years I have been diagnosed with the illness, I have found it harder to meet someone as a partner and also to have a quality relationship with anyone in life because of what goes along with it. What I mean by that is that when meeting people, it is difficult for me to interact with them, because I have found issues with many people in life that I can not control. Also, I have found many different types of people to be judgmental against others who don't fit the perceived definition of normal.

When I was young I never had these problems; I was simply introduced to people in life and I didn't really worry about what effect I was going to have on them. I simply lived my

life as a child, without much responsibility. I
have found that as I get older, it has been
more difficult to find the right people to spend
time with, and those that seem to be able to
hang out, can't because they have their own
responsibilities.   As I went through high school,
I found that girls became harder to get along
with and found it to be more difficult to find
the people that I would like to allow into my
life.

Other relationships I have had
throughout my life would be close relationships
like my mother and father who have been
there for the entire time. When I have needed
someone to turn to as a young person, or even
as an adult, I have found that they have been
there for me along the way. I can't
hypothesize about relationships that could
have been or might have been, but what I can
do is discuss the ones I know are a part of my
life. Strong relationships include my mother

and father and grandparents and close cousins. Weak relationships would include girlfriends, co workers and schoolmates.

I suppose in recent years I have had a more difficult time meeting someone that is worth spending time with or someone of value, due to reasons of judgment or simple problems of communication. For one, in the real world I have been born into, people work and live their lives, and I have learned that it is not that these people don't have time to spend, it's just that they have their lives and responsibilities that makes it difficult to do so. When I was a young person, I would get a chance to go hang out with my neighbor or friend from school, for a little time each day. As I have become older I have noticed that these hang out times are fewer, due to the responsibilities people have. People go their own ways and I have to just deal with it, and understand.

I would play and play all day during the summer months all by myself. I spent a lot of time as a kid outside and checking out what things were and getting involved with my own things. I would play basketball, I would play video games; I rode a bicycle and I played in a tree house. I miss having some of those things today, but I try to spend time with my dog, who is my companion friend, and I like to get outside and I enjoy doing things that get me active. I have been trying to find people that would like to do similar things I do, like hike, walk a dog, or cook. I think that is the difference from when I was younger and now. There really wasn't access to the social world we have today. I would just meet people at school, or I would meet people at a job or a volunteer opportunity. There would be kids in the neighborhood I would be friends with, and I suppose it is still the same as it was back then, it is just me who needs to take action.

Since leaving New York, I have lived in a small apartment community where there are a variety of residents that if I wanted to talk I could. I have found that what I want to do sometimes is just have basic friends that I can rely on, and perhaps have a girlfriend who I can be there for and her for me. I have found that it really doesn't turn out that way though. Again, there are many differences between life as a young person and as an adult, and one of those is responsibilities. I have found that if you are not a responsible adult that most people don't want to have much to do with you. A job has been an important thing to have as adult. It shows people you are responsible and wins you friends and possibly a girlfriend. But over the years, it has been difficult for me to find someone to create a life with. I feel sad sometimes as I can't and don't have any control over it. In my adult life I have had times with a job and career that has led me to places where there was a possibility of

becoming someone other than a poverty
ridden adult. I have found that leading a life
as an actor led me to places like large cities
where I had the chance to become someone.

What a person needs, are relationships
to make their life what it is supposed to be. A
person cannot exist entirely alone, without
friends. But I have found that a relationship
with God has changed a lot of that, as in truth
you are never alone with God. That is
something that helps me through tough
situations. Living with God has helped me,
above all, make it through many situations,
and I probably didn't even know God was
looking over me during those times. What I
wish, of course, is if I could just find someone to
spend time with in the future, to grow and
meet a nice woman again who would spend
the time. It is difficult when you have a
mental illness or disability and a woman wants
to know where the money is coming from. I

think money has a lot to do with it, however, and I think people in general want to know that about me when we meet.

Over the years, what is interesting is I really have never had any lasting relationships. There have been a few when I was younger, but they ended for a couple of different reasons. I hadn't been diagnosed with a mental illness yet. I have found out that women want a man that is serious, and if you aren't then they turn their head. I have also found that the women I have come into contact with aren't always the best people. I have found that there is a lot of baggage that some women carry with them, especially at my present age. I am a little wrapped up in online dating, because I have found that I don't want to go out and meet someone at a local church and be the guy that is prowling for women. I don't think I am that type really, but I guess church is not really the place to meet someone.

I have found that there aren't really places one can go just to meet people, and I have found that the online dating seems to be an answer to that.

When I was younger certain technologies didn't exist, and I would be outside for most of the day anyhow. I never really thought of meeting someone and to have children until I was in my twenties; however, I found that when I was working most of the time, I never really had the chance to meet anyone anyhow. A couple of relationships I have had ended because of the time difference, or things would end because the other person cheated on me. I have only had that happen once, but it sticks with me. I have had other relationships which were quality relationships, but when I had to leave for work or money, they ended. I suppose things happen for a reason, but sometimes I feel that if they were meant to work out, that they would; however I don't want to attribute the last four years of my life, not having a relationship with anyone, because of my battle with schizophrenia.

There have been a number of other reasons, but I have been given a lot of perspective while I go about life alone, just as there are many people who have families and relationships and even children. I don't. Just before coming back to Colorado, I had a short relationship with a woman in New York. It ended because my finances were low and I had to leave the city. She then went off and found someone else to marry! But I couldn't control her as I can't control anyone in my life. I can only control my own actions. This I know to be true, but I can't do much about others. All I can do is attempt to pursue them to befriend me and perhaps that will lead to a relationship.

Voices

When it comes down to it, I really don't hear voices. I think there was a time when I saw some nasty stuff in my sleep and felt very paranoid about people, places and things; however I never really heard voices. I feel that I have heard things in different settings, like when I go someplace, I have a fear that people are plotting against me, and have some thoughts that when I go out to eat, that people are eating my name, but I never actually heard voices that I thought were actually speaking to me telling me to do something. I can say that I have felt that the refrigerator talks to me in the *voices* of women, and that I have had some interesting dreams about people, about men and women doing funny things, but never have I been on drugs and *I believe* it all to be normal. I have found that a lot of what I hear, whispers and such, seem to have been television or radio programs.

I have seen television from a young boy and I have watched less and less recently. In fact, I have had thoughts of selling it all for the money. I would rather have cash in my pocket sometimes than a television that is just begging me to watch it. But it doesn't talk to me like that of some horror film. I do feel like I have been quite paranoid about people and their intentions, which I can attribute to the illness I suppose. I am on medication now, and I have noticed that I always feel a little better after a good night sleep and I can safely say that I have been rested. I heard a story once from a woman at my NAMI group who said that she was ever so happy to find a soft, clean and safe place to sleep at night, but that she too never heard voices.

Thoughts are different than voices. I will say that I have had some irrational thoughts in the past that sent my mind into a few different directions. It never got so serious that it kept me from functioning or something else. I mean, I have heard stories about people in disarray from the voices they hear in their heads about murder or irrational actions toward other people. I have never had such thoughts. There have been times that in looking out for my personal safety, I have been able to find ways to keep myself safe and have thoughts pertaining to safety and responsibility, but that I believe to be normal when moving to a new place. If I think about it more, I suppose I used to hear voices or thoughts as others would respond to me as I live. In other words, in certain places, I used to hear voices that were positive and reaffirming in my actions, for work, and for any other things that I would do. For example if I cooked a meal for myself and then ate it, I would hear voices that say, "He's eating." I think the voices are more in line with thoughts and actions that coincide with one another. I believe that comes along with people that I am close to or around. I think it may happen more often as I live around real people, as their responses are to the actions that I carry out. The voices come when I am in action.

Most of the voices, if I ever have heard anything, have been reaffirming in my life thus far, which is good. Except for the television, I believe that any voices that have come to me and have persuaded me to do something or not to, I really have not had much experience with that. When I have read about people with schizophrenia hearing voices, it has usually been delusional and persuasive to do some kind of harm to another. I understand that people have aggressive feelings toward others at times in life, but I recognize that it is never grounds for something violent. I think to myself, all I need is a problem with the law.

When I have had treatment in my sessions with a psychologist or a psychiatrist, not once has it come up where I have heard irrational voices in any regard. In fact I am usually complaining about something else or describing other types of problems I am having associated with the illness. The voices I hear are usually real voices of people who I believe to be talking about me in some negative way which in fact doesn't seem to be the case once I look and listen to the actuality. I am older now, and can usually take the drama at hand and disregard it, because of its non importance, unless of course there is reason to feel like I should focus on it.

I suppose if I hear anything it usually is people's judgments against me or what I do, and it then lingers in the air and it is up to me to take it seriously or brush it off. In that regard, it happens regularly if I listen to the cars outside. I can hear voices in the cars out on the streets, and sometimes if I listen close, I hear the judgments and discussions of others, but it is never so much that it persuades me to do something dangerous or irrational. I think of voices like those of a bad neighbor who forces you to throw rocks or to vandalize the local supermarket or steal from a neighbor. I don't have those kinds of thoughts, as some do, when short of money or out in a bad neighborhood. I think these voices that I have heard so much about, have come to persuade some people to steal from a bank, to steal a car or to break in to someone's house and steal a television. I have never had these sorts of thoughts. It is sort of like when you get around a group of people who have alcohol and they are all drinking, then it is your choice whether or not to have a drink of your own when, in fact you have the choice to disregard or to join in. I suppose the voices take on that sort of nature. When and if they ever were to kick in, I can see how these people or voices could be persuasive enough if I was in dire need of money, food or anything else.

I can see how the voices that present themselves would be as answers to the questions that one could have, but in recalling if I have every experienced anything of that nature, I really haven't. For me, it has been thoughts that put me into a different mindset, that push my thoughts into a different direction that I wouldn't have thought of. For example, I have been on disability insurance for a little over a year now and I have noticed that it has helped me in some way be more stable, and to not have to go out and get money every week, find a job, become nice and cordial when I need to be. It has helped me remain stable without the assistance of other people or jobs that they provide. I have experience in different areas in life as well, so this experience has lended itself to helping me with conquering the bad thoughts and attempting to do something that puts my mindset in a better direction. I have noticed that positive entertainment is good with helping me get out of my own thoughts and get into a storyline or something entertaining. Music helps with conquering any negative thoughts I have as well. I find that music soothes many areas of my mind.

Basic entertainment helps with the thoughts I have from time to time and helps me see what else is out there, but I do find that simply focusing on a paper like this or writing a short story helps focus my mind into a more productive area than "getting money," even though I think about that quite often. I find that doing something like reading and writing or something like math helps me be more productive and I feel that it is a good way of getting out of the mindset that I have an illness or have something to worry about. I keep busy in a number of ways and making my life productive with different activities helps me focus on what is important by not letting my mind scatter to something that is not helpful or won't do me any good. As far as hearing voices or thoughts of persuasion that tell me to do one thing or not, I have not experienced anything that has manipulated me in any way. I may have thought some things from time to time that are a direct result of my situation financially or socioeconomically, but I don't find these thoughts to be counterproductive.

Animals

This year, after nearly fifteen years of not having an animal in my life, I went to the local humane society and I picked out a dog. I figured, I was disabled, I had enough money coming in to have a dog and I wanted a companion that I would be able to spend time with and do things with. I ended up going to look at puppies, because I wanted a puppy and not a full grown dog and so I adopted a little puppy. I spent a little more money than I should have, but in life I have found, everything costs money. I picked up a Fox Terrier breed and it is a smooth coat type. I bought him in January of 2016 and I have been hanging with him since. I spoke with my mother and she picked out a name: Buster.

I have found that Buster has been a source of positivity for me as well as a challenge. I have found that I needed someone to spend time with, and for me, to spend time with a dog, without worrying about what it thought of me, what kind of reaction it would have to my illness, I have found him to be a good friend so far He was a year old in October. So far, he is a spoiled dog, and gets fed twice a day and sleeps a lot of the time. It is nice to have him around, because I can go out on a walk, I can hang out with him inside, and I can talk to him and play. After the initial cost, I have a chance to spend time with him for free, and it is something I like to do, because taking a walk doesn't cost any money.

Money continues to be a problem in my life, however having an animal has helped shift my mind away from the thoughts of money and has kept me active and less of a lump. I do feel that there is a good relationship between Buster and me, but sometimes I want to have some more freedom back because I want to get out and do some things that I feel for some reason I can't do while having the responsibility of a dog. It is a definite responsibility and I have enjoyed the different things that go along with having an animal in my life.

I believe Buster has helped me get out of my own world a bit and put my attention on caretaking. However there are times I don't want to take care of him or have him at my side, but then I really can't do anything now that, as my family and friends are saying, I made up my mind and got him when I did. Now he is mine for good. Buster is a good friend. That is unbiased and he hasn't a judgmental bone in his body. He sleeps a lot of the time and then on the weekends or a free day, we will go to a park close by and throw the tennis ball and run together. I have found that he is a nice dog too and even tempered. I have noticed that there are a lot of different tempered dogs out there and it was good to come across a dog that was warm and calm, in a world full of crazies. He is small and fits the size requirement for the apartment where I live, where they allow dogs. I have been set up with a disabled card that I can use anywhere, as Buster is now registered as an Emotional Support Animal. I have a little card for my wallet that I can show to a potential place where I would live if I needed them to accept my animal to live with me.

Buster is black, brown and white. He has a white belly and a black back. He has brown markings all over and two above the eyes. He has tall ears, which have reminded some people of a Doberman pinscher. When I adopted him he was listed as a Smooth Fox Terrier Mix. He has a smooth coat, and the other type is wired hair, curly and such. I am not sure what he is mixed with and I asked at the time of adoption, but the Humane Society couldn't tell me. So, we spend time together regularly and I write at home; I clean or take care of chores around the apartment and he hangs out with me.

When I got him, I ended up spending more money than I wanted, and I got a small kennel to keep in my apartment as I needed a place for Buster to sleep at night, but it turned out to be too small. One day, as I was passing by my neighbor's door, she popped her head out and said that her dog had died and that she would be happy to give me her old dog kennel that she had for her dog. I told her I would give her a dollar for it and she said I could have it for free. It was almost twice the size as the old one I had bought. So, I ended up returning the first kennel to the store and keeping the kennel from my neighbor.

So, in a sense I have had a good connection with the dog so far this year and he has become one of my only friends in this world. I bought a little collar for him and a leash, both which are the color blue. He continues to be a little friend of mine that I can simply hang out with and he does not have any biases. I do believe that he has helped me get through tough times and it is nice to have something to care for, an animal that I can call a friend.

In the past, as a child, and in my adolescent years growing up, I have had other animals. I had a fish tank in my younger years and also in high school, and then I had a couple of different dogs, one that I remember particularly, a Chow Chow named Einstein, who was a strong influence on me and was also a good friend. I enjoyed having a fish tank and also I liked having a dog that I could spend time with, one that would comfort me and I could play with. It was nice to have a family dog that was warm, generous and sweet, and wasn't mean.

After all of this, I would say, that for me, being diagnosed with an illness, I have found that having an animal has greatly increased my quality of life through months that may have been bad and not happy. The dog has brought me joy to times that I don't normally think of things being joyful and I have found that just simply having an animal around greatly increases my positivity about life. Although I think about moving from time to time, and if I did, wondering if I could take my dog with me, I am happy to say that I have a companion now that helps me through each day.

Life and the Future

Over the course of the last couple of
years living with schizophrenia, I have begun to
notice changes to the overall quality of my life
when I am able to pay my bills and not yell
and scream for money every time I run out.
The disability has helped me survive in a better
way than before, and even though, I have
never really held a job that paid very much, I
have found that a disability benefit, while not
that much, does help with primary expenses,
thankfully. Over the past couple of years,
when I was struggling to make anything, I
found that moving to Colorado greatly helped
me get out of a place of trouble, and into a
better place that was safer and cleaner and
healthier. I took it for granted growing up, but
I have come to realize that nothing should be
taken for granted: the times you spend in
other places, meeting people or enjoying

nature. Over the course of the time in Colorado, I have come to recognize the goodness of life.

While I was in New York, I found that it was a serious struggle for a lot of people including myself, and while living there I found it to be even lonelier than it is in Colorado. I can say that I had secluded myself even more in New York as an actor and that moving to Colorado, in a way, opened me up a bit. I still find myself alone a lot of the time, but I think there are chances for me to get outside and about more often now than before. When I have lived in other cities, I was there for work primarily and I was always working to get my career going. Looking back, while I am back in Colorado for an extended period, away from a career that is based on song and dance, I have found myself to be more collected and stable now than before. I don't have the desire to get up in front of a crowd and sing and dance any longer. Now, however, I find there to be an easier way of life for myself where I can simply think clearer in a state full of sunshine and cool mountain air.

Looking back even further, I see myself in argument with the people and places I have been and the jobs I have worked at, and I still to this day have issues with the system and way people go about their daily lives. I simply try and stay out of harm's way as I am able to have a little money in my pocket because of the disability. I would have to be on my own in a job if I didn't have a disability and in this market I would absolutely have no job. The world is getting more and more difficult to survive in and I can say that I have made the decision to find an inexpensive place to live where I can survive. If I was to live in a larger city, God knows there would be higher expenses and I would have to worry about getting proper medication and keeping a sound place to live. Currently I find myself in a safe place that isn't too expensive, where it also keeps me out of the spotlight of the rest of the world. Before, I always had a desire to be on stage and screen and I recently have turned to writing and it has been a good creative outlet for me.

There are differences in how I live today from how it was years ago when I was a struggling actor, but I found that it became more and more difficult to become an actor when a person's finances are low. If you aren't working in a job, then you aren't working. It is that simple. I have found ways of survival here in Colorado, but it hasn't been easy, however. Having this disability has given me the room to breathe, whereas before I was struggling to get my head above water.

My life now is much better than it used to be, but in a sense it is the same. There are changes that I have gone through while seeking help and getting the proper mental health care I needed. There has been sort of a trade off, as I have stopped working for the companies that exist out there, but I have been living off of the disability, which has been helpful to me mentally. It has kept me from burning out my life going back and forth from place to place trying to find work and dealing with people when I don't have the desire to be nice or to perfect their order as a restaurant server or a retail representative, or to clean the bathrooms in a tourist destination, or to get on the phone to try and raise money for politics. I have found that living on my own time has helped me survive better and kept my mind clearer.

Once thing that hasn't changed is the chance I would like to have to meet someone special to add to my life. I haven't had the chance to really meet someone that wants to spend time with me. Too much work, and not enough play. It was nice to be in a larger city and to work in a place far away from my hometown, but I have found that over time, it was just money out the door to people that I really didn't know or care about. It turned out that I was spending more money than I was making, and as an actor and artist, this is important to realize. In any city, I am sure it is difficult to survive if your income is lower than your expenses, and just living in a smaller town I have begun to realize that people still don't care about anything but money to get to their bottom line.

I hope that the treatment I have received has helped me, but in a general sense I know that it is me who needs to help me and I want to make sure I come to a place where I can help myself, and not be reliant on others to help me get out of the ways I am in. I can say that over the past few years I have been a

better person, I have got out and volunteered
in the world, I have tried to help the elderly
and lived a little less hasty. I have always had
to watch my spending wherever I go because
there are people who are trying to take my
money everywhere. Now, being on a fixed
income as a change from before, I have to be
even more aware of my spending. I think that
is something I have had to be conscious of for
most of my life, as I have never made enough
money to pay my bills and live comfortably. It
has always been that my spending
overshadows my income.

So, here is to a new life. One where I
am not in treatment can make my own
decisions and am able to say I have some
friends and can keep out of trouble. Over the
years I have worked at a number of different
service-oriented jobs which have led to
nowhere. I can honestly say that there were
days that all I thought about was money and I

couldn't get anything else done. At least now, I can survive a little better while I work on my stories, my writings and try to complete some poetry. I like to stick with something creative as it gets me out of my head and onto the page. Before, I was acting, playing roles and characters and although acting still holds a place in my heart, I can only do so much as I have found it better to write and create something original which is my own, instead of acting in someone else's world and production. I find that I would rather create something from nothing than rely on other playwright's words.

For now, I have shifted my life to creation and writing, instead of acting and producing. In the past ten years I have been in different productions as an actor and even though it is my chosen profession, I have found that being out of work is really no one's fault but your own. So I have chosen to write currently to get myself out of working for other people. It has helped me focus my energies into a story, a plot and characters. So far I have been writing short stories and poems, and currently I stay creative by writing something when I have the time, and staying by myself, out of the eyes of the critics in life. As far as my mental health, I have found it interesting, and difficult, but rewarding when I come up with something that is my own creation. After this, I hope to work on many different projects that keep my mind healthy and active, and myself out of the trouble out there.

In the future I hope to stay working and writing things that keep me interested and focused on what is important. Short stories and poems don't pay the bills unfortunately, but I have now been working on books that I can sell. In the future maybe I will work on something that I can say has been sold or even helped someone out there seeking guidance form someone who has had the experience. That might be possibly the most important part of writing this book; helping people with my words would be a good reason to write. I can say that it is important to help myself in the process. I hope that in the future I can sell some books, become a published author, or create a play based off of some of my ideas as I continue. I don't have forever, and I haven't settled on a play idea yet, but I hope that in the future, when I get to that project, that I can come up with something worth reading. As far as the mental health, it continues to be something I work on daily and stay on top of as I have been able to be more productive in my thirties so far, more so than in my twenties. Schizophrenia has been just another hurdle I have had to jump over and conquer, but in life it continues to be something I work on and try to keep the voices at bay.

Acknowledgments

I would like to thank my family and God for helping me daily through my projects and work. I also would like to thank my close friends and neighbors who have been there for me through the years and have helped me though these tough times. Thank you to those that have helped me through my suffering. Thank you, the reader, for your support.